WHAT YOU CAN DO NOW

EVEN WHILE YOU ARE STILL IN SCHOOL, there are many steps you can take to prepare for a career in television production. Speech, drama, English and art classes will allow you to develop your creativity. Some high schools have their own broadcast facilities, so volunteer to work off-camera to get some experience with the visual and sound components involved. Classes on filmmaking, mass media, writing, and photography can also be helpful. Becoming computer-savvy is essential, as most TV studios run their operations with special software. If you are unable to find the right classes at your school, look for courses at a local college, through professional organizations, and online.

Spend as much time as you can learning the craft of producing television shows, commercials, films, plays, and other types of productions. Online courses and YouTube videos provide a close-up view of the artistic and technical aspects of video and TV presentations. Watch TV shows – not just for entertainment, but also as research. Notice how programs are structured, how the camera moves among the actors, and how the cinematographer arranges shots to create the desired impact. Study classic TV shows like *I Love Lucy,* and notice the basic sitcom rules that are still applied today. Then analyze sophisticated dramas on HBO and A&E. Many colleges and cities host film and video festivals. Volunteer to work at the festival, and you may meet working professionals.

Anyone who plans to work in television should read trade periodicals, visit professional association websites, and follow industry blogs to stay up-to-date with industry trends. Such print and online publications as Variety, Hollywood Reporter and Broadcast & Cable can provide valuable insights into the industry. Professional organizations often have useful practical information on their websites for industry workers.

Get involved in your local creative community. Join a film club, theater group, audio-visual club, or similar organization that can help you build skills to use in a TV production career. Similarly, independent television and video productions often welcome unpaid volunteers to staff their projects. Newspaper ads or your state film commission may lead to local productions needing help – maybe even a paid part-time job.

HISTORY OF THE CAREER

IN MANY WAYS, THE TELEVISION INDUSTRY evolved from the performing arts media that preceded it, such as theater, radio, and cinema. Many careers in television – producer, director, writer, actor – are similar to those in other media, but with television, technology has been a major driving force throughout the industry's development.

While there were inventors working on devices to transmit moving pictures in the mid-1800s, the early breakthroughs with mechanical televisions were not commercially viable. The first television demonstration came in 1926 in Scotland. Bell Laboratories followed up with an American version the next year. The world's first television station came in 1928 – General Electric's W2XB in Schenectady, New York. However, the early mechanical TVs had limited capabilities and faded to black in the 1930s.

In 1927, Philo Farmsworth demonstrated the first electronic television in San Francisco. Electronic televisions used beams of electrons to scan images and project them on a screen, the basic principle still used in TV sets today. At that time, radio was the dominant entertainment media, broadcasting live drama, comedies, news and sports around the world.

CAREERS IN

TELEVISION PRODUCTION

MANY OF THE MOST EXCITING, LUCRATIVE and prestigious careers available today are available in television production. The field includes producers, directors, cinematographers, writers, editors, camera operators, special effects experts, and sound engineers. Many TV professionals work at studios and production companies in the major entertainment centers of Hollywood and New York City. Others are employed in smaller cities, creating local news programs, morning talk shows, instructional videos, web-based video series, and commercials.

Could you be successful in the television industry? Talent – creativity, imagination, the ability to tell a good story – is an important qualification. Add some training on the technical and artistic aspects of TV, supplemented by practical experience as you learn the business, and you will be ready to start. Do you enjoy the creative process? Could you work well in a collaborative environment, teaming with fellow creative workers to guide a show from initial idea through broadcast? Can you handle constructive criticism? Are you persistent? If so, you could be successful in a TV career.

A four-year degree is not required but is typically helpful to get started. Some TV professionals start out in film school, but others get their training from traditional colleges and universities. A degree in TV production, journalism, or mass communication will give you a broad overview of the industry. More advanced technical training will be required for certain specialties, such as camera operator or sound engineer.

TV professionals work for major production studios, local television stations, corporations, not-for-profit organizations, marketing firms, and advertising agencies. Some are employees of production houses or studios, working as part of a team that creates each week's episodes for a series. Others are contractors who move among different studios to tackle individual projects.

It is not easy to break into television, as competition is fierce for the limited number of positions available. There are about 130,000 positions available in television productions, with average annual earnings of about $70,000.

You will need talent, training, and determination to succeed. If you are willing to spend the necessary time studying the industry, learning the basics of TV production, you can achieve the personal and professional satisfaction that accompanies a career in television.

RCA, the dominant radio company through its two NBC networks, set aside $50 million to further develop Farnsworth's electronic televisions. By 1939, RCA was selling television sets and began regular TV broadcasts in major cities. CBS, the main competitor to NBC, began its TV broadcasts in 1941. Also that year, the Federal Communications Commission ruled that RCA must sell off one of its networks. That unit became ABC, which began TV broadcasts in the early 1950s. The "Big Three" networks would dominate the television industry for decades to come.

The TV pictures of the late 1930s were still relatively poor, and by the early 1940s, there were only six experimental stations broadcasting. World War II delayed further work while RCA and other companies turned their attention to military projects. It was not until 1947 that better TV sets became available and the networks started rolling out television broadcasts across the country. Radio was still the dominant mass media platform, but CBS and NBC earmarked part of their radio profits to improve television. Results followed quickly. The number of black-and-white TV sets in homes grew from 6,000 in 1946 to 12 million in 1951, and they were found in half of all American homes by 1955. The Emmy awards were introduced in 1949 to recognize excellence in the television industry.

The 1950s were considered the first "Golden Age of Television" as the medium established its unique character. Early shows had been mostly visual versions of popular radio programs. Then, in the early 1950s, the networks drew from the theater world to launch a series of popular dramatic anthology series (such as Playhouse 90) with original scripts. These programs employed veteran radio writers, actors and producers who created high-quality TV programs. Variety shows, game shows and situation comedies were also introduced, along with numerous creative and technical innovations. Many shows were broadcast live, while others were filmed and edited like movies. The first videotape recorders were put into use by TV stations in 1957, enabling many formerly live programs to be recorded on tape.

However, the editing process was cumbersome, as editors had to use razor blades to cut and splice the physical tape. Increasing competition among the three networks for the viewers that drove advertising dollars also led them to abandon many of the sophisticated, highbrow plays they presented in favor of more popular comedies, dramas and action shows that appealed to broader audiences.

In 1964, the networks introduced color TV programs to capitalize on newly-commercialized technology for capturing, broadcasting and receiving color images. Improvements in sound and new cameras for color TV shows required increasingly sophisticated operators, lighting technicians, and audio engineers. By the 1970s, film and video editing entered the computer age with the first non-linear video editing equipment. The 1970s also saw the US government create the Public Broadcasting System, a fourth national network that offered educational programs and the high-quality programming that commercial networks had largely abandoned.

Cable television was the next trend that challenged the networks' dominance of the television industry. While cable had originally been used to bring broadcast signals into geographically isolated areas, it spread across the country in the mid-1970s as a source of additional programming. Home Box Office (HBO) began offering recent, uncut movies in 1975. It was followed quickly by cable stations TBS (old movies and sitcom reruns), ESPN (sports) and the 24-hour news station, CNN. These cable companies later began creating their own original content, drawing viewers away from the traditional networks.

DirecTV, founded in 1990, and other satellite broadcasting services soon followed, offering an alternative delivery system for cable and broadcast shows. Despite the emergence of Fox as a fourth major TV broadcast network in 1986, the future lay with cable stations.

By the late 1990s, television sets evolved further with high definition (HDTV), a new standard that provides almost cinema-quality pictures. The low-definition traditional broadcasts were replaced by digital television. The spread of personal computers in the late 1980s, the rise of the Internet in the late 1990s, and digital television, combined to set the stage for a convergence of television and the Internet in the new millennium.

That convergence was a major factor in what is being called the New Golden Age of Television, which began in the mid-2000s. Digital television, mobile technology, new cable channels, and the Internet drove the demand for more alternatives to the major networks. YouTube, which started as a video sharing site for amateur productions, soon attracted creative artists who produce high-quality short videos for mass consumption. HBO was the first channel to invest in original high-quality programming, and its series *The Sopranos* (1999-2007) launched the new Golden Age. HBO was followed soon by such cable competitors as Showtime and A&E. Netflix, an Internet-based streaming video service, and Amazon, began producing their own series to supplement their movie and TV libraries. Other services like Roku and Hulu provided access to libraries of network programs and films.

Today, the large volume of high-quality TV programming across a vast array of smartphones, tablets, computers, and Internet-connected devices provide the television industry with more choices than ever before – and more opportunities for talented professionals to work in the industry.

WHERE YOU WILL WORK

THE MAJORITY OF TV PRODUCTION PROFESSIONALS WORK in studios, as most recorded programs and live broadcasts are created in facilities where lighting, sound and other conditions can be controlled. Editors, sound mixers and others work in offices and editing suites filled with high-tech equipment. However, some TV production work must occur outside the studio, such as broadcasts of sporting events or live news feeds, and outdoor scenes recorded for TV dramas.

Most TV production personnel work for one of the broadcast or cable networks, at local stations affiliated with those networks, or at independent studios. However, television production can also be done at advertising agencies, nonprofits, corporations, government agencies, and other companies of all sizes. These organizations create informational videos, presentations, advertisements, video games, and infomercials. The companies can range from small firms that employ a handful of professionals to global media conglomerates. While the most visible positions are found in the entertainment capitals of Hollywood and New York, other TV production staff members live and work in cities of all sizes across the country – particularly at local TV stations and advertising firms.

Still, most of the TV jobs are in major metropolitan areas with strong entertainment industries. California is the top state for employment of producers and directors, followed by New York, Texas, Florida, and Georgia. The metropolitan area with the most jobs for producers and directors is Los Angeles, followed by New York, Atlanta, Washington, Chicago, Philadelphia, Boston, Seattle, San Francisco, and Miami. California and New York also lead the nation in employment of camera operators, sound engineers, editors, and other positions.

Most of the 95,000 producers and directors employed work in TV and radio broadcasting. Many are employed in motion pictures and video, and a smaller number work at advertising and public relations firms. The TV, film, and video industries are also the top employers for announcers, camera operators, sound engineers, editors, and similar production workers.

Employees at TV production studios typically enjoy some of the best working conditions in any industry. They have clean, comfortable, safe offices located in state-of-the-art facilities that offer the most current technology. TV production requires a collaborative group environment, with offices where creative and technical personnel work together to create programs. However, camera operators, audio/visual engineers, reporters and others who work on location may be exposed to severe weather conditions and hostile surroundings. Camera operators and their producers must be able to carry heavy equipment when in remote locations.

Freelance production personnel are not employed by a single company, but rather move from one organization to the next to work on a particular project. They may work at a studio, in company offices, on location, or in some cases, from home. Established freelancers may retain an agent to help them find work. Freelancers also find jobs through networking, industry publications, or referrals.

THE WORK YOU WILL DO

THERE ARE A WIDE VARIETY OF ROLES you could play in a television production. Some are extremely technical in nature, such as camera operator or sound engineer. Others are largely artistic, such as director and cinematographer. Most career paths demand both technical and creative skills to work in the highly collaborative environment of television.

TV professionals may be employed directly by a network or a local station. They may work for a production studio that creates programs for a network, or an advertising agency that makes commercials. They may also work for corporations, government agencies, or not-for-profit groups.

In general, TV production work falls into three categories that represent the life cycle of a live or taped television show: pre-production, production, and post-production. Some roles span more than one, such as producers and directors who are involved throughout the project. Also, some phases may overlap – such as a special effects animator creating images before the show is taped.

Pre-Production

Pre-production covers all the activities before shooting begins. This phase includes writing the script, hiring cast and crew, arranging financing, building sets, designing wardrobe, and creating a production schedule. Writers, costume designers, and casting agents are active during pre-production.

Production

Production is the actual work to record the TV show – or, in the case of a live event, to broadcast the program as it happens. The production phase covers setting up the studio (or the outdoor shooting location) with the proper electrical, sound and lighting equipment; selecting camera angles; applying actors' makeup and hairstyles; fitting costumes; rehearing scenes; and recording audio and video feeds. Assistant directors, production assistants, lighting and sound technicians, cinematographers, actors, and hair and makeup experts work during production.

Post-Production

Post-production refers mainly to recorded shows. It includes editing footage shot during production; adding music, sound and visual effects; mixing audio tracks; merging sound with images; additional reviews and edits; and final approval of the show. Editors, special effects artists, sound designers, and composers are primarily active during post-production.

Producer

Producers are primarily charged with making the business decisions for a TV series or broadcast. They initiate, organize and manage all aspects of producing live and taped television programs through the phases of the TV show life cycle. They pitch ideas for shows to networks, obtain financing from investors, create the budget, hire the director, and compile the production schedule. Producers are multitaskers who need to know all the roles in the TV industry and how the business works. Creativity is required to select the right projects and find novel ways to overcome the challenges of each project. They also need to demonstrate sound leadership, money management and communications skills. Producers may have to resolve creative and personal conflicts to keep the project on schedule and within budget.

It takes years of experience in the entertainment industry

and a successful track record to become a producer. Many start out as actors, cinematographers, assistant directors, or screenwriters. Their typical career path includes production assistant, and sometimes more technical roles to gain a broad knowledge of the TV industry. For live television broadcasts, the producer is present in the control booth, overseeing each night's show, coordinating commercial breaks, communicating with on-camera talent, and making sure the program stays on schedule.

In addition to the main producer on a TV show or series, there are numerous variants of producer titles that generally carry less responsibility than the full producer. The executive producer is the most common type. For some production houses, the executive producer is the highest-ranking person involved in daily activities. Other shows may have multiple executive producers, many of whom are not involved in the day-to-day work. They may have limited duties, such as hiring cast or securing funding. Sometimes the title is merely honorary, as in the case of stars that appear in the show.

Beyond the executive producers, line producers take care of financial matters and budgets. Television commercial producers create advertisements for paying clients. Co-executive producers and supervising producers are often writers or supervise the writing staff. Field producers are in charge when filming occurs outside a studio. Edit producers and post producers are active in the post-production phase. TV newscasts also have other types of producers, such as a segment producer responsible for one portion of a longer show.

Production Assistant

Working as a production assistant is the most common entry-level position on the producer career path. A production assistant may perform a variety of tasks on a show, ranging from fetching coffee to running script revisions to the cast and crew. Production assistant is commonly a lower-wage position at local TV news operations. An assistant TV producer or associate producer has more responsibility than the production assistant, but duties still vary widely. They may help update scenes in the script, revise dialogue, or set up camera shots.

Director

While producers focus on business considerations, directors bring the creative and artistic vision of a TV production to life. They help choose the cast, oversee set design and wardrobe, tweak the script, and outline the production schedule. During shooting, directors work closely with the actors, cinematographers, lighting technicians, audio engineers, and prop masters to make sure the scenes are filmed properly and correctly.

For a live broadcast, such as a sporting event, the director tells the camera crew what images to show, and selects what sound and video goes out while the broadcast is underway.

In post-production, the director helps editors, special effects teams, and sound engineers make the right artistic decisions to support the director's goals for the TV show.

Like producers, directors can come from a variety of other TV disciplines and bring years of experience to their role. They may start as writers who want to direct their own scripts, as actors who want more control over their work, or as production assistants who have worked their way up to greater responsibilities. There are also various types of assistant directors, with duties varying from running errands to directing second units shooting supplemental scenes such as backgrounds.

Program Creator

While producers and directors are common in films and theater, the role of television program creator is unique to TV. The creator is the person who comes up with an idea for a program, pitches it to a production studio or TV network, and maintains some role in at least the initial shows. Creators often start out as writers, directors or producers.

Showrunner

In many cases, the creator becomes the showrunner, a person responsible for a TV series' daily operations. Showrunners are responsible for the "big picture" view of where a TV series will evolve over a given season. They report directly to the producer, TV network, or production company. Showrunners have the highest degree of creative control – even outranking the director, who may or may not be the same person during the entire season. One example of a successful showrunner is Nic Pizzolatto, who started as a scriptwriter for network television. He created the series *True Detective,* sold it to HBO, and served as executive producer and writer during its first two seasons.

Other Production Roles

While producers, directors, actors and writers get much of the media attention, there are many other TV production roles that are critical to a successful show. Some of the main positions include:

Cinematographers, camera operators, and videographers (or directors of photography), place the cameras, determine shooting angles, and direct the camera operators to film or tape the scenes. Camera operators and videographers may work in the studio or in the field, particularly when covering breaking news.

Electrical, lighting and sound workers, set up the various equipment needed. Lighting specialists and electricians have such titles as gaffers, grips and best boys. Boom operators place the microphones off camera, while sound engineers monitor the quality of the audio recording.

Makeup, hair, and wardrobe workers make sure actors' appearances match their role on the show and the director's artistic vision.

Casting directors help the director screen and select actors for roles. They often know just the right actor to play a particular part.

Art directors are responsible for the overall visual look and feel of a production, including set decoration and props.

Prop masters (short for property masters) buy or make the physical elements needed for a production, such as weapons or furniture.

Editors take the raw footage shot during production and assemble it to create a finished TV show. They combine shots from different camera angles and ensure that the transitions between the scenes are smooth and make logical sense to the viewer.

Visual effects artists add images that were not part of the original footage, such as explosions. Most special visual effects are generated by computers and added to the show during the editing process.

Sound editors and designers function like visual artists, except that they create new sounds that are added to the program. Foley artists create physical sounds (such as using coconuts to mimic a galloping horse).

Composers create music that is added during editing.

Multimedia artists and animators create special visual effects for TV.

Announcers add narration to a prerecorded program, or they may speak during a live broadcast (such as sportscasts).

The exact duties and responsibilities for any of these roles may overlap in a given TV studio or on a specific show. However, all of the television professionals work long hours to bring the technical and artistic vision of a TV show to life.

STORIES OF TV PRODUCTION PROS

I Direct Sports Broadcasts

"Since I was a kid growing up in Texas, my two great passions have been photography and sports. I played everything my parents would let me sign up for: football, baseball, basketball, soccer, lacrosse, and tennis. But as much as I loved to play, it was soon obvious I would never be a pro athlete or even a collage player. I was usually second or third string on my high school squads, but still happy to be on the field with some occasional playing time. When I wasn't competing somewhere, I was busy with still cameras, film, and soon videos. I created short videos and posted them to YouTube. I originally planned to become a videographer, a cameraman, or maybe a magazine photographer, so I went to college to study visual arts and creative technology.

I found what would become my true calling at the University of Texas in Austin. Even though I only played intramural sports, I was always hanging around the varsity teams and shooting images. One day the football coach asked if I would be willing to videotape the practices for him. Of course, I accepted! The assistant coaches told me what shots they wanted, and I complied. Soon I was traveling with the team and shooting their game films. I quickly developed the instincts and split-second timing required to anticipate where the plays were going and how the game was flowing. My volunteer work helped our team improve – and gave me some great clips for my portfolio. I also met working broadcasters and camera operators when the big TV networks covered my games, and I made sure to cultivate those relationships.

After graduation, I used many of those contacts to line up interviews with local TV stations and sports networks. I landed an entry-level job covering high school games for the Fox affiliate near my West Texas hometown. After more training and a couple of years' experience, I was able to move up to the Fox Sports Southwest network as a full-time sports cameraman. This regional network covers all types of college and professional sports across Texas and surrounding states. A few more years, and I became an assistant director. I guided the other cameramen to get the best shots for our broadcasts. Last month, I became a director, which means I'm supervising three assistant directors and selecting which shots go out in the live broadcasts. It's a new challenge I'm just starting to sink my teeth into, but already, I'm enjoying the excitement of sharing my love and knowledge of sports with our viewers."

I Am a Television Cinematographer

"I did not start out planning to work in television production. In fact, I wanted to be a musician. I started playing guitar in junior high and joined my first band at age 14. My friends and I played music at parties throughout high school and college. I knew that the music business is tough, so I didn't really plan on a full-time music career. Still, it was plenty of fun during my younger years and provided an artistic outlet.

In college at the University of Georgia, I decided to major in mass communications, thinking I could use my music as an entry to a creative career. One of my bandmates wrote music, and we built up a library of new songs. We decided a couple of music videos would help us promote the band locally and online, so I asked a classmate who was a video major to help us out. I worked with him as a second cameraman on the project, and I found I had a knack for camera work. I took more courses on filmmaking, videography, editing, and camera techniques. We soon started a small business working with other bands on their videos and live concert footage.

After college, I moved back to Atlanta and found there were already several production houses working on music videos. However, I also found there were entry-level opportunities in television at CNN, the global 24-hour news network based here. I began as a production assistant – basically a "gopher" who fetched copy and ran the Teleprompter. It gave me a chance to work alongside the camera operators and learn their skills. It also inspired me to take some technical classes to learn more about how to operate the video cameras.

While my time at the news operation was a great learning experience, I didn't really want to spend my career in a studio shooting images of newscasters. Fortunately, CNN is part of Turner Broadcasting (which is owned by Time Warner), and there were other TV operations in Atlanta where I could work on original programming for TBS, the Cartoon Network and Turner Classic Movies. Within a few years, I worked my way up to the leader of the camera crew and eventually director of photography – the title we use here for a cinematographer who oversees the entire visual shooting process.

At Turner Studios, I've done lots of work in the studio and in the field. I really enjoy the creative challenges of using images, camera angles, lighting and camera movement to tell the director's story. Don't get me wrong – I still play my music on the weekends – but cinematography is my true creative outlet."

PERSONAL QUALIFICATIONS

REGARDLESS OF YOUR SPECIFIC ROLE IN TELEVISION production, you will be involved in telling a story. You may work on news reports, dramatic series, or promotional videos. Whether you serve as producer, director, cinematographer, or sound engineer, you must be able to use images and sounds to bring the narrative alive.

Effective TV production is a craft, requiring technical and artistic skills. To get started, you do not have to know all the technical details of jobs beyond your own, but you will need a general knowledge of what everyone does on the production and who is responsible for which duties. Over time, you will learn the roles each contributor plays.

It takes a diverse group of people working together to create every TV program you see, so being a team player is mandatory. That means you must be able to collaborate and communicate well with others, both verbally and in writing. You must be able to give and accept constructive criticism, as artistic disagreements among team members are common. Ultimately, when the discussion is over and the producer and director make a decision, you must be able to put aside your own artistic vision to implement the team's point of view.

It can take a long time to build a successful career in TV. You will need patience, self-confidence and persistence while you build your portfolio and work your way up in the industry. This is a highly competitive business, so keep your ego in check and develop a tough skin.

Project management and team leadership skills are also important for producers, directors, production managers, and others with similar roles in the production. Leaders create and monitor schedules to ensure deadlines are met, and the entire team must be able to follow those schedules. Producers must also be able to determine which projects have good prospects for success, how to hire the cast and crew, and how to allocate budgets for the production.

Good computer and problem-solving skills are also important for all types of TV production roles. Other useful traits for TV personnel include reliability, sound judgment, a responsible attitude, creativity, an open mind, flexibility, sound organizational skills, originality, professionalism, self-management, and a high personal code of ethics.

Throughout your career, you will need to keep learning. If you are in a highly-technical role (such as sound engineer or camera operator), you will need in-depth training on the latest equipment and technological developments. Everyone should study industry trends by reading trade magazines and industry sites online.

ATTRACTIVE FEATURES

TELEVISION PRODUCTION OFFERS numerous choices to pursue a prestigious and satisfying career, providing opportunities for self-expression, as well as above-average compensation. Working at a network television studio – or even the local TV morning show – can be a glamorous, exciting opportunity where you spend your days alongside creative professionals. Developing a television program is a collaborative process, so you can work with a variety of interesting people. This is one of the few careers where you can see your own ideas come to life on screen. Fame typically only comes to actors, directors, and producers, but the entertainment industry offers prestige to everyone who works in TV and affiliated media.

Most employees at television networks, local affiliates, and production companies work in clean, well-lit, modern offices or broadcast studios. They use state-of-the-art production equipment and other modern technology to do their jobs. The industry offers a range of career versatility and new challenges every day. If you work at a remote shoot, you may be outdoors filming a dramatic episode for later viewing. Or you may be at a sporting event, relying on satellite feeds or streaming video to broadcast the game to fans around the world. Whether in the field or in the studio, you will be using the latest technology on a daily basis.

Some TV production personnel are employed by a single network, TV station, or other production facility. However, many experienced professionals become freelancers, moving from studio to studio as new projects begin. They enjoy many of the same benefits as TV staff receive, including a competitive salary. If you are a field producer for a news or documentary series, for example, you may be sent to exotic locations around the world, leading a team of reporters and audio/visual technicians reporting on current events. If you like sports, you may be able to direct the broadcast of your college football team's big games.

Most of the high prestige and high earnings TV production opportunities are found at major studios in California and New York, so many television professionals live and work in those areas. However, there are opportunities in other cities as well. Local television stations, advertising agencies, independent video houses, corporations and nonprofit organizations also need TV production staff. You may not be working on *Game of Thrones*, but the industry still offers opportunities to build lucrative, satisfying careers in your own hometown.

UNATTRACTIVE ASPECTS

A CAREER IN TELEVISION PRODUCTION is likely to be demanding and stressful. Regardless of your exact job title, expect to work long hours to meet aggressive deadlines. If you work on a TV series, there is a new show every week during production season, which means script reviews, rewrites, rehearsals, shooting and editing. At a local TV station, you may be chasing breaking news or juggling schedules when a studio guest cancels an appearance. Ad agencies and corporations that produce commercials are constantly hustling to create the next video advertisement. Keeping the creative juices flowing over a long period of time can be exhausting.

The first and longest battle is often simply breaking into the TV industry. The profession requires talent, training and making the right connections. Even established freelancers go through "dry periods" when they may be out of work for months at a time. While TV production can eventually provide a steady income and a secure career, it can take years of working your way up the ladder to achieve that.

Producers and directors in particular must prove their abilities through a series of responsible positions before they are entrusted with major projects. The ultimate responsibility for a TV program's success or failure often falls mainly on the producer, director, and leading actors. The TV industry can be glamourous and lucrative, but it still requires hard work to get ahead. Producers face financial risk if they back a project that is not profitable or that draws poor ratings.

Television is a collaborative media, which can be frustrating. You are one voice among many working on a project. Many others can and will dismiss your ideas in favor of their own. TV writers and showrunners work on large teams where fellow writers, producers, directors, technicians and actors have input to the finished product. You may sell most of your colleagues on a concept, only to be overruled at the last minute by the director's creative vision.

TV production personnel of all types need to continually improve their craft and keep up with new trends (both in technology and in popular culture). This can require taking additional courses and workshops, and attending conferences; reading trade magazines; and following online news on the television industry. The use of mobile technology and social media also presents new demands for technical savvy. Even on-air newscasters are under pressure to post constant updates on Facebook, Twitter and other social media sites to draw viewers.

The number of new TV production jobs is generally not increasing quickly, so competition for openings is expected to remain stiff. Freelancers in particular must constantly be looking for the next project they will work on once their current assignment ends.

TV production is usually a physically safe career with few injuries, with most work done in a studio or an office rather than at a remote location. However, the stress, long hours and irregular schedules can encourage unhealthy eating habits and interfere with your personal life. Frequent computer use can also cause eyestrain, back pain, and other injuries.

EDUCATION AND TRAINING

WORKING IN TELEVISION PRODUCTION requires a combination of technical and artistic skills, which are developed and enhanced during years of education. You can get a good start in high school by learning the basics of television, video, theater, computers, and the use of technology to enhance visual storytelling.

For most television production roles, you typically need at least a four-year college degree. However, a two-year associate degree is often sufficient for positions that are more technical. Attending a film school (an institution that focuses on creating visual entertainment for TV, video and movies) or an art school can be useful. However, you can also pick up everything you need to know in a traditional school. In fact, there are thousands of colleges and universities that offer TV-related degrees. Graduate degrees, such as a master's or doctorate, are not required unless you plan to teach at the college level.

Some schools offer a specific television production major, but others include TV in a broader context that includes film, online video and other media. Many television professionals obtain a liberal arts degree, with a major in mass communications, English literature, film, theater, or journalism. Regardless of your major, take as many classes as possible to learn about the production world. Volunteer for extracurricular activities where you can develop those skills. Create a "reel" (today usually a DVD or even your own website or Facebook page) showing a portfolio of your best work.

You may have only a general desire to work in TV but have not focused on a specialty yet. Many people move among fields in college and even in the workplace before they settle down in one area.

If you plan to become a producer or director, you may benefit from a bachelor's degree with a major in media production. Those roles demand knowledge of all the jobs involved in television production. If you are going to direct a camera operator, for example, you need an idea of the capabilities and limits of what a camera can do under certain situations. Common college majors for producers and directors include film/cinema/video studies, radio and television, directing and theatrical production, dramatic/theater arts, and cinematography and film/video production.

While many colleges and universities offer degrees in these and related areas, future producers and directors often choose to attend film school. These institutions cover the television and motion picture industries with such topics as the history of mass media, editing, lighting, and the creative aspects of making a TV show. At any school, these professionals will complete classes on television broadcast management, journalism, writing, editing, communications, and current technology.

If there is a particular part of the industry where you want to work – such as editing for an animation studio – find schools where you can focus on that specialty. If you want to produce the nightly news, you may pursue dual degrees in journalism and TV production.   Broadcast sound engineers, cinematographers, and editors need detailed training in the technology required to do those jobs, so they must ensure their school program gives them hand-on experience with the newest equipment. While film is still used for some television shows, digital cameras and editing tools are the most common media, and the technology is constantly evolving.

If you prefer to attend film school (or an art school with strong visual communications programs), some of the best-known and highest-rated are:

University of California, Los Angeles (UCLA)

New York University (NYU)

University of Southern California (USC)

American Film Institute Conservancy

Columbia University

Wesleyan University

University of North Carolina

University of Texas at Austin

Loyola Marymount University

University of Wisconsin/Milwaukee

Ringling College of Art and Design (Florida)

Savannah College of Art and Design

Other programs that provide training in TV production may focus strictly on television; on TV and radio; or on video, film and broadcasting. The largest broadcasting production schools by student enrollment in the United States are:

Arizona State University

Miami-Dade College

University of Florida

University of Central Florida

University of Texas at Austin

Michigan State University

University of Arizona

California State University

University of Houston

Temple University

San Diego State University

University of North Texas

University of Georgia

San Jose State University

Boston University

Wayne State University

University of Tennessee

With so many choices, how do you pick the right educational institution for you? Start with national rankings of film schools and universities, which are available online. Use these surveys to narrow your options, and then visit the websites of individual schools to learn more. Look for opportunities to gain hands-on experience creating work samples to expand your portfolio. Also decide whether you need a Bachelor of Arts degree, or an Associate of Science in a technical field to get started.

An internship during or immediately after college is an ideal avenue for gaining practical work experience, honing your technical and artistic skills, and networking for your first job. Your college or film school may provide access to internship opportunities with local production companies. A number of websites also serve as clearinghouses for TV production internships, such as InternMatch.com.

Once your TV production career begins, you must continue your education and training. There are always new skills to learn and new techniques to explore. For example, the increasing demand for 3D entertainment is creating the need for more professionals knowledgeable in this specialized area. Even if you are not in a highly technical role, you still need to keep up to date on which TV shows are popular and what new Internet-based media platforms are being introduced.

EARNINGS

ANNUAL EARNINGS IN THE TELEVISION production industry are on average about $70,000. Salaries for producers and directors in all types of media average $100,000. The top 10 percent of producers and directors earn $150,000 or more, while the bottom 10 percent receive about $50,000. Most directors and producers work in radio and television broadcasting, which pays an average annual salary of about $75,000. However, the top paying industry is the motion picture and video sector, which pays an average over $150,000. Other top industries for employment include cable and other subscription programming, advertising and public relations, performing arts companies, and sound recording firms.

Assistant TV producers average $30,000 to $50,000.

Recent surveys by Glassdoor.com found the national TV producer salary averages about $60,000, while PayScale.com reported film and TV producers average $65,000 per year.

For camera operators in the TV, cinema and video fields, the average annual salary is $55,000, with the top 90 percent receiving $95,000 annually. Television broadcasting employs about 5,500 camera operators who earn an average of $45,000, second only to the film and video sector – 7,700 employees and $63,500 in annual pay.

About 8,000 cinematographers earn an average of almost $95,000 in California, with New York ranking second with almost 4,000 jobs and almost $80,000 in pay.

Broadcast and sound engineers receive annual wages of almost $60,000.

California is the state with the highest employment of producers and directors (24,500), sound engineers (4,000), camera operators for TV, video and film (4,500), announcers

(2,900), plus cinematographers, video editors, and others. New York ranks second in most categories, with other top states including Texas, Florida, Georgia, Illinois, and Tennessee. Los Angeles and Hollywood are the top metropolitan areas for TV production professionals, followed by New York City.

Experience, training, and location are major factors in pay rates. Freelance TV professionals generally earn more than their peers with salaried positions, although they may also be out of work between contracts (which typically run one year). However, all types of TV professionals work long and sometimes irregular hours against strict deadlines.

OPPORTUNITIES

EMPLOYMENT IN THE TELEVISION INDUSTRY is expected to grow in the coming decade at roughly the same rate as the total for all occupations – about 11 percent. However, that figure varies among specific types of TV careers, ranging from just a small increase for producers and directors to almost 15 percent for audio and video equipment technicians.

For directors and producers, industry experts foresee modest growth for TV, video and film producers and directors. Production companies are experimenting with new content delivery methods, such as mobile and online TV, which may lead to more work opportunities for producers and directors in the future. Projected employment of producers and directors is estimated at just over 100,000 within the decade.

In more technical fields, camera operators and cinematographers for TV, video and motion pictures are expected to see a slight rise in employment to about 22,000.

Employment of film and video editors will remain essentially flat at about 28,000. Broadcast and sound engineering technicians will see good increases in employment to over 130,000, with broadcast technicians accounting for about a third of those jobs.

While most opportunities will remain in the traditional media centers of California and New York, the number of TV positions is also expected to grow in other parts of the country. For example, generous tax incentives in states such as Georgia and Louisiana have brought several new studios to those states for production of movies, TV series, documentaries, music videos, and more. Advertising and public relation firms also rely on TV and video skills to produce commercials, interactive media, streaming web videos and other materials for their clients. The booming Internet traffic in original videos (particularly on YouTube) is driving demand for professional-grade productions there. Opportunities to move into new media outlets can be found in most cities and states across the country.

Overall, as the television and online video production industry continues to expand, the demand for TV professionals will continue growing. The additional need for creative and technical artists to work on interactive productions, advertising applications, video games, mobile phone apps, the Internet and social media will also increase for years to come.

GETTING STARTED

ARE YOU READY TO PURSUE A CAREER in television production? Making the decision to become a TV producer, director, writer, announcer, cinematographer, camera operator, sound engineer, or special effects creator is an important first step. Do not wait until you finish college to get started. You can take action now to begin preparing for your future career.

Start by gathering more detailed information about the different types of production roles available. Then determine what steps you need to take to work towards your specific goal. You can find written information about career options at libraries, from colleges and universities, and through your school's career center. The Internet has a wide range of easily accessible data from industry websites, TV networks, media companies, government agencies, and other groups.

Before beginning college, find ways to get experience in TV production – either at school or in the community. Seek internship opportunities, volunteer positions, or entry-level jobs, particularly with TV stations or independent video makers. If you want to make TV commercials, contact an advertising agency. There are also plenty of local and online courses where you can learn new skills. Whatever you work on, build a portfolio of your work that demonstrates your experience.

A four-year degree is generally needed to get started in the TV industry, so determine which film schools, art schools, colleges and universities can provide the training you need. Make sure they have programs that focus on the television industry and the particular job you want to land. Look for internship opportunities, plus outlets to create an impressive body of work that you can send to potential employers.

Spend some time talking to people working in television.

Ask what skills and experience they look for when considering applicants coming out of college. You can find these individuals through professional associations or local production companies. Industry associations can also be helpful for learning about the profession, local career opportunities, internships, training programs, and scholarships.

Do not forget to rely on your personal network for support and advice. Discuss your plans with family and friends. Also include your school counselor who can provide helpful information about educational venues, employment prospects, and networking outlets.

Once you gather your data, it is time to give careful thought to whether a career in television production seems right for you. Are you comfortable with both the creative and technical aspects of TV production? Do you work well with others in a collaborative setting? Can you put in long hours to meet deadlines? Do you work well under pressure?

The most important factor at this point is whether you can visualize yourself happily pursuing a successful career in the television industry. If so, start taking those first steps today towards a rewarding, fulfilling career!

ASSOCIATIONS

■ **Academy of Motion Picture Arts & Sciences**
http://www.oscars.org

■ **Academy of Television Arts & Sciences**
http://www.emmys.tv

■ **American Cinema Editors (ACE)**
http://www.filmeditors.org

■ **American Society of Cinematographers**
http://www.theasc.com

■ **California Film Commission**
http://www.film.ca.gov

■ **Directors Guild of America**
http://www.dga.org

■ **Independent Film & Television Alliance**
http://www.IFTA-online.org

■ **Motion Picture Editors Guild**
http://www.editorsguild.com

■ **Music Video Production Association**
http://www.mvpa.com

■ **National Association of Broadcasters (NAB)**
http://www.nab.org

■ **National Endowment for the Arts**
http://www.nea.gov

■ **Producers Guild of America**
http://www.producersguild.org

■ **Pro Video Coalition**
http://www.providevideocoalition.com

■ **Screenwriters Federation of America**
http://www.screenwritersfederation.org

■ **Society of Broadcast Engineers**
http://www.sbe.org

■ **University Film & Video Association**
http://www.ufva.org

PERIODICALS

■ **ACE Magazine**
http://www.filmeditors.org

■ **Broadcast & Cable**
http://www.broadcastingcable.com

■ **Broadcast Beat**
http://www.broadcast.com

■ **Daily Variety**
http://www.variety.com

■ **Deadline Hollywood**
http://www.deadline.com

■ **Editors Guild Magazine**
http://www.editorsguild.com

■ **Filmmaker**
www.filmmakermagazine.com

■ **Huffington Post**
www.huffingtonpost.com

■ **Post**
http://www.postmagazine.com

■ **Produced By Magazine**
http://www.producersguild.org

■ **The Hollywood Reporter**
www/hollywoodreporter.com

■ **TV Guide**
http://www.tvguide.com

■ **TV Technology**

http://www.tvtechnology.com

■ **TV Week**
http://www.tvweek.com

■ **Video Maker Magazine**
http://www.videomaker.com

WEBSITES

■ **A&E Networks**
http://www.aenetworks.com

■ **ABC Talent Development**
www.abctalentdevelopment.com

■ **CBS Corporation**
http://www.cbscorporation.com

■ **InfoComm International**
http://www.infocomm.com

■ **Interactive Advertising Bureau**
http://www.iab.net

■ **Intern Match**
http://www.internmatch.com

■ **Museum of Broadcast Communication**
http://www.museum.tv

■ **Television Academy Foundation**
http://www.emmys.com/foundation

■ **Television Writers' Vault**
http://www.tvwritersvault.com

■ **The Pulitzer Prizes**
http://www.pulitzer.org

■ **TV Internships**
http://www.tvjobs.com/intern

CPSIA information can be obtained
at www.ICGtesting.com
Printed in the USA
LVOW13s1503060717
540470LV00014B/774/P

9 781523 241330